My DEPRESSION

Copyright © 2005 Elizabeth Swados

All rights reserved. No part of this book may be used or reproduced in any manner whatsoever without the written permission of the Publisher. Printed in the United States of America. For information address Hyperion, 77 West 66th Street, New York, New York 10023-6298.

Library of Congress Cataloging-in-Publication Data

Swados, Elizabeth.
My depression: a picture book / Elizabeth Swados.—1st ed.
p. cm.
ISBN 1-4013-0789-2
1. Swados, Elizabeth—Psychology—Pictorial works. 2. Authors, American—20th century—Biography—Pictorial works. 3. Depression, Mental—Patients—Biography—Pictorial works. 4. Composers—United States—Biography—Pictorial works.
I. Title.
PS3569.W1TZ47 2005
818'.5409—dc22
[B] 2004060223

Hyperion books are available for special promotions and premiums. For details contact Michael Rentas, Assistant Director, Inventory Operations, Hyperion, 77 West 66th Street, 11th floor, New York, New York 10023, or call 212-456-0133.

First Edition
10 9 8 7 6 5 4 3 2 1

To Drs. Loren Skeist
and Julie Spain
my beloved tour guides

And to Roz
because.....

Special medals to: Amy Gross, Charlotte Sheedy, Kelly Notaras, and Bob Miller, who are great soldiers in the Army of Ink.

Lincoln- thanks for teaching me about cartoons.

MY
DEPRESSION

What a great life I have!

I write music ♩ ♫

Plays

Books

(And actually make a living . . .)

I have two giant
chocolate-colored poodles . . .
(and a tiny white Bichon)

Colleagues I respect

Loyal and lovable friends
and lovers

Talented students
and performers I
adore

But it all gets cancelled out

When I get into a depression.

I've had depressions off and on
for most of my life

Teens   Twenties   Thirties   and onward . . . . .

At times it's felt like we're a pair

It's not any consolation, but I know
I'm far from alone. Too many of us
communicate from down here.

Here are some of the things that start a downward spiral...

Seasonal change

Rejection or humiliation

The World

Loss of family
or friends

1921 - 1974

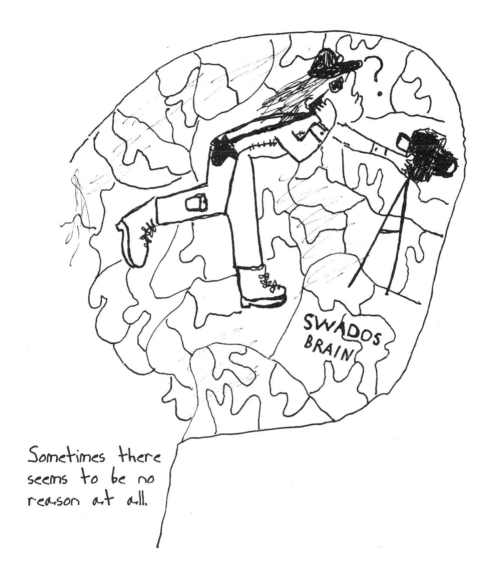

SWADOS
BRAIN

Sometimes there
seems to be no
reason at all.

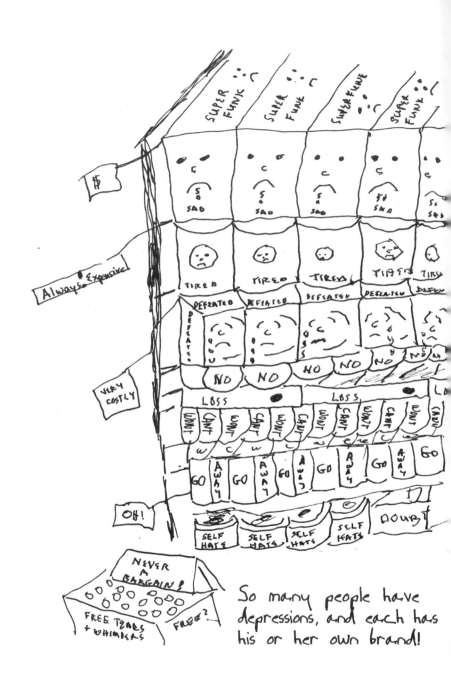

So many people have depressions, and each has his or her own brand!

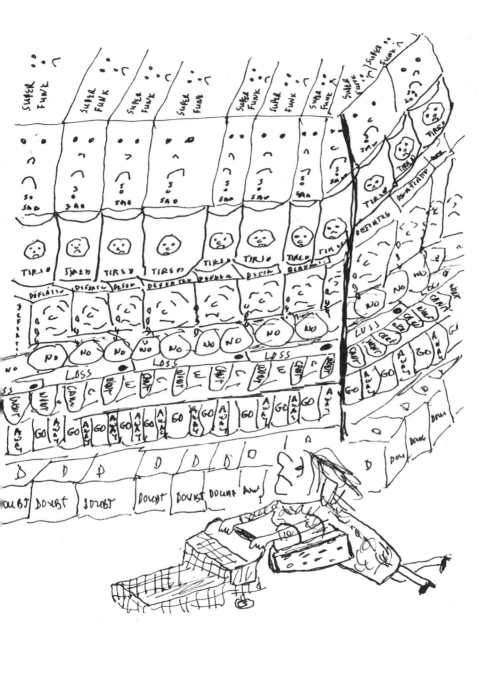

But I know my own best.

My depression begins with a little cloud at the edge of my vision.

I only sense it's there.

Soon the cloud is accompanied by
a buzz and a whine ——
Suddenly I can only write
sad songs.

People say, "Liz, this is a musical comedy."
But sad songs are all I have.

The cloud gets bigger
and grayer, the
BUZZ louder.

Now none of my music sounds good.

The words I've written are mundane,
bizarre, or incomprehensible.

I start leaking confidence.

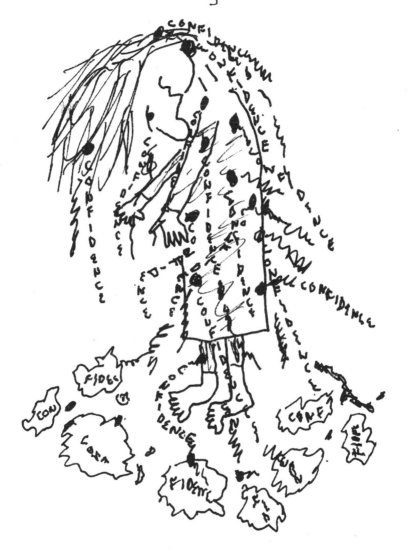

I begin to hear every word that every negative critic, professional or otherwise, has said or written about me.*

*not verbatim but chillingly close.

I'm blind to all the good things.

I'm snappish and short-fused,
provoking the worst out of
those I love best.

My own self-loathing gets transferred onto others.

I tell a friend that her new makeup makes her look like a drag queen playing a geisha girl.

I stand up my editor because I decide his bowtie is pretentious.

I tell a singer she sounds like Ethel Merman on heroin.

There is nothing worth learning ! ५"

I cancel classes because "they don't want to learn anything anyway"

BICHON

I tell one of my dogs to "go feed herself"

The small crimes build...

I avoid friends by telling them how successful and busy I am.
"I have 3 operas to write. Two movie scores. A commission for B'nai B'rith. I'm doing meetings with folks from Disney. I'm teaching creative drama at NYU. I'm writing an article for Vogue on girls and math. I've got an unbelievable new lover. A concert at the Maryknoll convent. My father's condo burned down in Boca Raton and I'm comforting him. Going to Africa to work at an orphanage. Setting the poems of Rumi to music. Teaching a street gang choral music...."
FINE
GREAT
SUPER

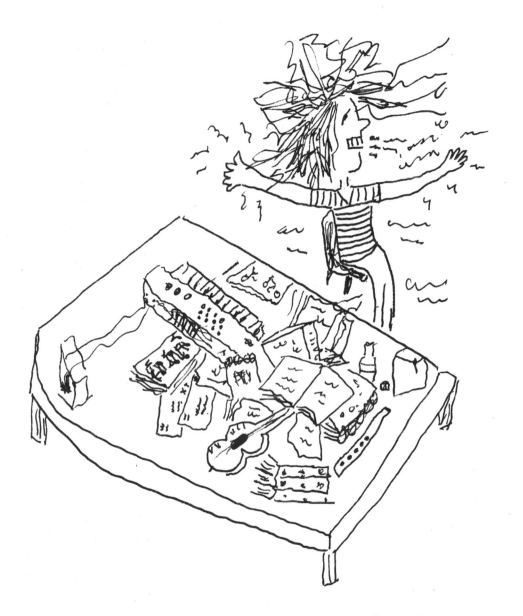

When, in fact, the idea of work terrifies me.

Why go out, when I've become so old, fat, and ugly?

I'm a pariah in my own mind. Something slimy
and scaly feels like it's growing inside me.
I'm a grade B 1950s horror movie!

When I'm depressed, things of the world conspire against me. I can't get anything right right right

RIGHT!

Then I start with outright lies... the tragic ones.

The truth is much more dull.

When I dare to go out I seem to run into people who are doing so much better than me.

*not verbatim, but chillingly close.

I get so buried in this mess of my life.

Friends try to help, but I keep them at a distance.

I often reject and insult them.

hidden
cloud

I worry that
people will find out
I'm depressed and
think less of me.

I feel their scorn.

That little cloud keeps getting bigger.

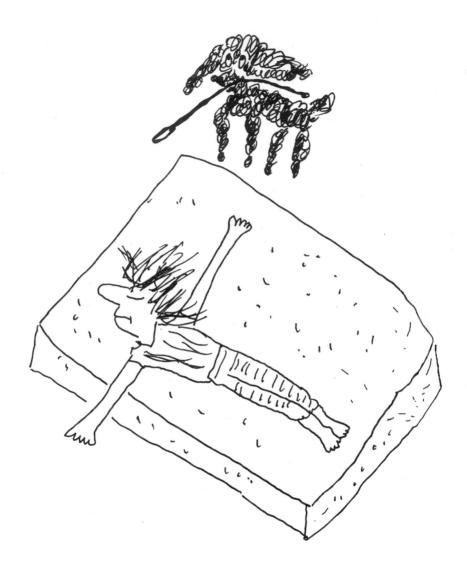

It gets harder and harder to get out of bed.

I take no interest in my life.
I can't clean my loft, take out
the garbage, or shower.

I start smoking.

The idea of food makes me sick.

Nothing's worth talking about.

Living with me is impossible
when I'm depressed.

Sometimes I self-medicate.

But it's useless because, stoned or sober...

The Courtroom still convenes in my head:

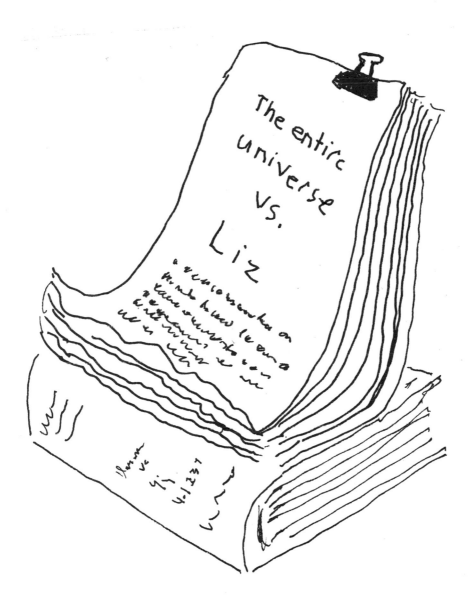

The Witnesses for the Prosecution
(there is no defense)

"Yes, I was her cleaning lady for 15 years. I'm seventy-five now. She sends me money but never does come to visit."

The Cleaning Lady

The Grammar
School Girlfriend

"We did everything together! We were friends since kindergarten. Now she's too hip for me. Doesn't return calls."

The Agent

"She's had seven music agents, five literary agents and three managers. Some at the same time. She's the first artist polygamist."

The Student

"She didn't send in my college recommendation. She _lost_ it!"

"She was my favorite. I did anything for her. But when she returned from Africa all she would do was sing these weird circumcision rituals from Mali and drum on the coffee table."

The Aunt

The Cousin

"Suddenly she calls and wants to be close, just like sisters. But then I don't see her for two years! _Then_ I get some cracked Balinese puppet and it's not even my birthday."

The Father

No! Wait!
My father is excused from this book!

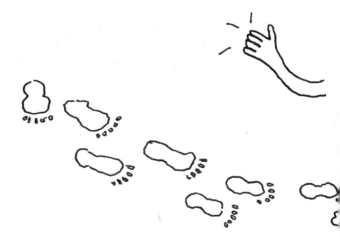

Now the two star witnesses

My mother, the suicide...

"YOU DIDN'T KEEP ME ALIVE!"

DIED AT 52

My brother, the suicide

"YOU DIDN'T KEEP ME ALIVE!"

DIED AT 46

Well, that hits a nerve.

I imagine we all have
one or two guest appearances
We could do without...

Now the deadened depression takes on new aspects

I'm flipping over into an agitated depression

At first
I'm terrified.
Then I'm angry.
I feel
paralyzed
but I can't
sit down
without
jumping up
or pacing.
Or twitching.
Or Falling.

This is bad because I think I am able to "function" in this agitated depression.

Once I cut a piece out of everything I owned and hand-sewed it into a quilted shirt for an Eastern European director whom I worshipped.

Luckily, he was as depressed as me so he saw it as a fitting tribute.

Most recently I wrote a 258 page novel whose leading character transmorphed into the following identities:

An ex-con from Bedford Hills

An ex-junkie dog walker

A punk rock cleaning lady who stole cleansers.

A dying philanthropist in Big Sur, California.

A child evangelist turned champion wrestler in West Virginia.

A psychic in the time of Houdini who wore no underpants

An FBI agent with an eating disorder.

I wrote it in 8 days.
No one will ever see it.

Aside from my obvious eccentricities,
I'm expressing a fundamental
underlying feeling that's
quite normal...

Anxiety makes me feel like I'm going to blow apart.

All I can think of is that I'll go nuts in public.

I rush out of posh restaurants because suddenly I can't feel my forehead.

Will I start screaming out loud in movie theaters?

Friends invite me to shows and I
walk out in the middle.

Anxiety turns to rage.

I kick
taxi cabs.

I lose all my compassion.

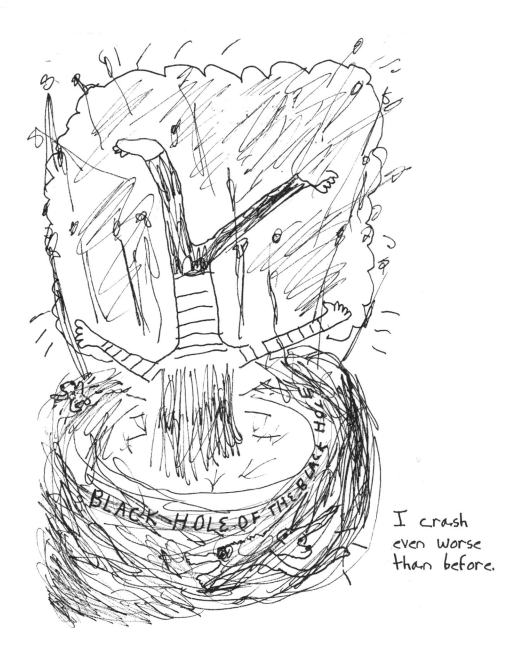

BLACK HOLE OF THE BLACK HOLE

I crash
even worse
than before.

I feel completely isolated.

I am tired of this multifaceted
and unpredictable depression

So are you....

But even
when I'm in
the depths,
there will be
a melody
or joke
that breaks
through . . .

A silly handwritten letter that's hard to ignore....

An oversized chair
and a tall friend.

But sooner or later,
the depression comes back.

Full force.

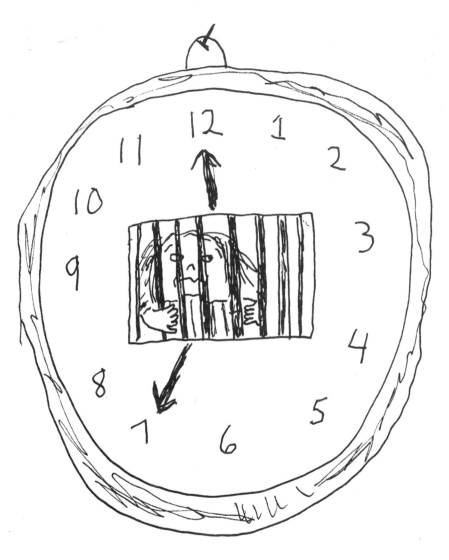

Each moment feels like it lasts forever.

The road becomes a
mountain that gets
harder and harder
to climb.

People begin to judge me.

Some still say there is
no such thing as
mental or emotional illness.

They're usually the super jock types.

Or secret alcoholics.

Or workaholics who hide
behind their briefcases.

or people born with a
natural ability to
function.

or TV gurus
with bestselling
books.

Those military types who believe a personal crisis is cowardly.

Or political people who call it unpatriotic.

DON'T BE FOOLED...

They're either lying or denying
or
they haven't been there...

On the edge of a black hole,
chased by a cloud of fear.

I have.

That place where you can't go forward
or backward.

At times, I have contemplated suicide.

As I've mentioned, my mother and brother chose that way out. Friends too.

Is suicide inherited?
Is it contagious?
Is it desirable?

Or is it just my family's way of solving problems?

They say the children of suicides are more likely to commit suicide themselves.

Will I ??

When I contemplate suicide, I think about famous people and their methods.

Virginia Woolf, stones in her pocket, walks into a river.

Kurt Cobain blows his brains out.

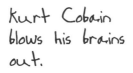

Sylvia Plath sticks
her head in the oven.

Mishima commits
Seppa ku.

I have a whole list of options:

YES	NO	
☐	☐	Hanging
☐	☐	Booze + pills
☐	☐	Death by cop
☐	☐	Driving off a cliff
☐	☐	Slitting wrists
☐	☐	Slitting throat
☐	☐	Heroin overdose
☐	☐	Bad mix of drugs
☐	☐	Attracting psycho dates
☐	☐	Plastic bag over head
☐	☐	Jumping off roof or out window
☐	☐	Long swim in the ocean
☐	☐	A dip in the local swamp
☐	☐	Attempting famous Houdini escape tricks
☐	☐	Fast motorcycle on greasy road
☐	☐	Other – please list

_____

_____

_____

Discounting, I think,
the buzzards and
scorpions.

And a certain lack
of knowledge about
what comes after.

But these are just
thoughts from the black hole.

The bottom
of
the bottom
of
the
bottom...

I want to be strong and consider methods for lifting the depression on my own.

I try . . .

Psychics

Forms of meditation, including breathing and chanting.

Herbal remedies

Yoga

Boxing

HEAVY BAG

Diets

Acupuncture

Regression Therapy

Massage

Punching
and
kicking pillows

Bio-feedback

Group therapy

Religion

Different possibilities, of course, appeal or
don't appeal to each of us.

Here are some of my personal recommendations:

Listening to a
CD of chanting
Tibetan monks.

Or the mountain women of Bulgaria

Reggae can sweeten your soul

So can Ella Fitzgerald's scat singing

Or breathing with a slow tango on the accordion

Some days I try to exercise.

Or at least walk from one room to the other.

Write down thoughts and feelings,
no matter how trivial or messy.

Read some poetry (most poets are depressives)

Watch animal shows, cooking shows and true crime stories through the night.

Look up "depression" on the internet...

Or if you prefer, "the effects of secret testing of the human brain by enemy alien scientists"

Cry your eyes out.

Let a piece of chocolate melt slowly on your tongue.

A good night's sleep can be very helpful

Fantasize about moving to a different country, converting, or getting extensive plastic surgery.....

But in the end, you know what they say—

WHEREVER YOU GO, THERE YOU ARE!

Eventually most of us
have to get professional help.
After years of struggle,
I did.

I had to look quite a bit before I found someone I could trust.

I met a doctor in a brown chair.

He had red hair.
So do I.
That was a start.

We discussed that severe depression is often hereditary.

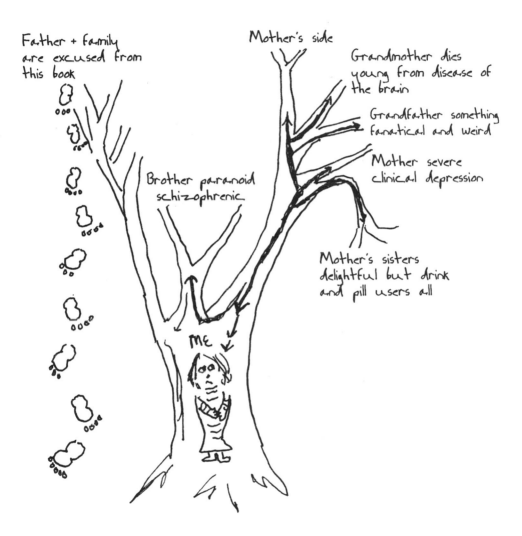

It's a well known fact that it passes from mothers to daughters. Hmmm...

The doctor said that part of my problem was chemical.

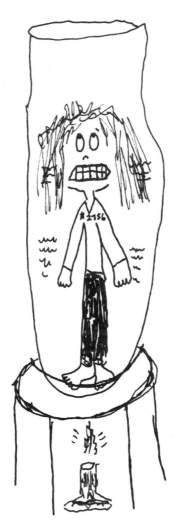

He asked me if I was willing to try some of the newest drugs that were coming out.

Thus began a series of medications.

You've seen the ads.

So many new pills. What do they do exactly?

Chemicals in the brain called neurotransmitters
or neuroregulators zap the parts of
the brain which
regulate mood
(or don't). Most commonly known are
norepinephrine, dopamine and serotonin.
When lacking one of these
chemicals, a person gets depressed.
So antidepressants
help make more neurotransmitters
so the brain will
naturally electrify itself

and rock on.

Think adrenaline.
Think endomorphs. (Only not.)

This is the space where
a qualified doctor corrects
my bogus chemistry lesson

_____

_____

_____

_____

_____

_____

_____

_____

The drugs help many, but not all of us and not all the time.

Sometimes they have side effects.

WARNING: This antidepressant may cause dizziness, vomiting, pain and self doubt, a longing for rye bread, bumps on your lover, invasions by South American revolutionaries, silly worms playing soccer in your throat, an inability to see the color blue, a bad tip in the stock market, a layer of cheese on the tongue, hallucinations of artichokes, turnips and ground chickpeas, bad taste in ties or shirts, a need to discuss your innermost wishes with the cleaner, stalactites or stalagmites (I can't remember which) hanging from your teeth, an overpowering need to become a DJ, sudden fires where you happen to have been, a sudden expertise at archery, the flowers you detest budding around you, an alarming risk of choking on dried-out brisket, now you can whistle but only wolves respond, obesity in goldfish, fungus, claiming you are Native American when you're not, the falling of the face, laughing, and yes, death.....

On one
combination
I decked a
drummer for
playing too loud.

(He _was_ trying to provoke me, but still...)

On Prozac anything anyone said,

day or night, night and day,

became a song from a made-up

musical comedy

Sometimes certain brands of anti-depressants have muted my sexual desire.

But I've learned you gotta hang in there.

It took around three years but
eventually we found something that
worked.

I found a good therapist who helped me learn to cope.

For a while, anyway...

Medicines can wear out or
go a little sour (like good coffee
or milk). You may have to
try another brand.

And even the best medicines
can't stop <u>life</u> <u>from</u> <u>happening</u>.

Depression can be a
one-time event.

Or you could be in for
a long haul.

12,256,83 miles

Either way...

You have to learn how to wrestle with it.

And hide it when you have to.

If you fake being positive, you may end up _feeling_ positive. Who knows?

You survive a little at a time.

Tasting
tomato
sauce

Hearing a
stupid bird
through your
window

Threading
a needle

Dousing yourself
with cold water

Sniffing a
new face
cream
(or hair gel)

Thanking the mailman for
the newest catalogue.

+ then reading it
cover to cover

Gradually, the little acts become medium sized acts.

"call back Ms. Tragedia!"

Listening to your answering machine.

Throwing out stuff from the fridge.

Turning off the T.V.

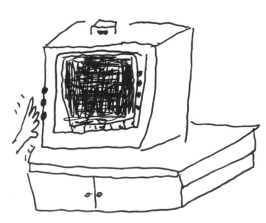

Making faces at a baby in a stroller.

They blossom into <u>bigger</u> <u>acts</u>.

Wearing something cheerful + sexy

Playing with a friend

Scratching a dog's belly

Eating a messy slice of pizza

Dancing to a boombox you hear on the street

Trying to understand why you feel as you do.

Reading about other people's depression.

Writing about your own.

SEE
THIS BOOK!

Getting past depression is big stuff.

You've won a bout.

Rebuilt broken parts.

Gathered little gems
of wisdom.

Got yourself
back together.

Maybe redesigned
your exterior.

What a victory when you start to come out of it!

Maybe you've learned
to look at things a little differently.

Learned to appreciate
what's right in front of
your nose.

Learned a little
compassion.

Learned to love
a little silliness
in others.

You might be interested in people and
enjoy them again.

Breathe in Life

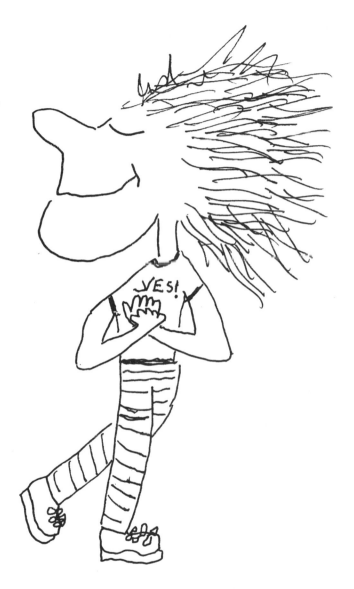

Maybe you've finally learned to love yourself.

What a relief!

Life is truly such a precious gift.

That little cloud may show up again.

Hopefully next time you'll be stronger.

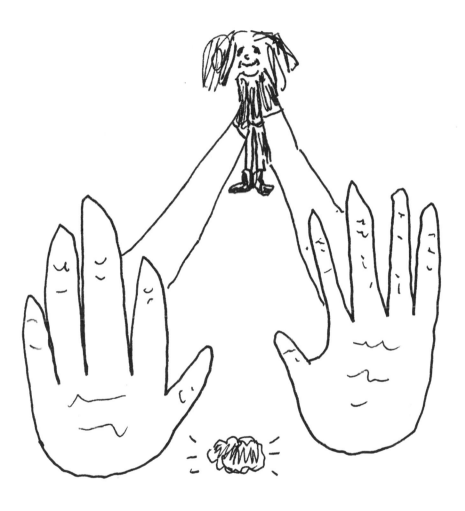

Remember, you got through once...

You can do it again.

The End